Day and Night

by Conrad J. Storad

Science Content Editor:
Kristi Lew

ROURKE CLASSROOM

www.rourkeclassroom.com

Science content editor: Kristi Lew

A former high school teacher with a background in biochemistry and more than 10 years of experience in cytogenetic laboratories, Kristi Lew specializes in taking complex scientific information and making it fun and interesting for scientists and non-scientists alike. She is the author of more than 20 science books for children and teachers.

www.rourkeclassroom.com

Photo credits: Cover © Joshua Haviv, Evgeny Dubinchuk, Cover logo frog © Eric Pohl, test tube © Sergey Lazarev; Page 3 © happydancing; Page 5 © Yuriy Kulyk; Page 7 © BirDiGoL; Page 9 © Heizel; Page 11 © vovan; Page 13 © nadiya_sergey; Page 15 © Andriano; Page 17 © Dolly; Page 19 © Lori Skelton; Page 20 © Andrejs Pidjass; Page 22 © Heizel, BirDiGoL, happydancing; Page 23 © Lori Skelton, Yuriy Kulyk, Andrejs Pidjass

Editor: Kelli Hicks

My Science Library series produced for Rourke by Blue Door Publishing, Florida

Library of Congress Cataloging-in-Publication Data

Storad, Conrad J.
 Day and night / Conrad J. Storad.
    p. cm. -- (My science library)
 ISBN 978-1-61741-724-5 (Hard cover)
 ISBN 978-1-61741-926-3 (Soft cover)
 1. Earth--Rotation--Juvenile literature. 2. Sun--Juvenile literature. 3. Moon--Phases--Juvenile literature. 4. Day--Juvenile literature. I. Title.
 QB633.S76 2012
 525'.35--dc22
                            2011003861

Rourke Publishing
Printed in China, Voion Industry
  Guangdong Province
042011
042011LP

www.rourkeclassroom.com - rourke@rourkepublishing.com
Post Office Box 643328 Vero Beach, Florida 32964

Did you know we live on a moving **planet**?

As the Earth turns, it changes from **day** to **night**.

The **Sun** rises in the East and sets in the West.

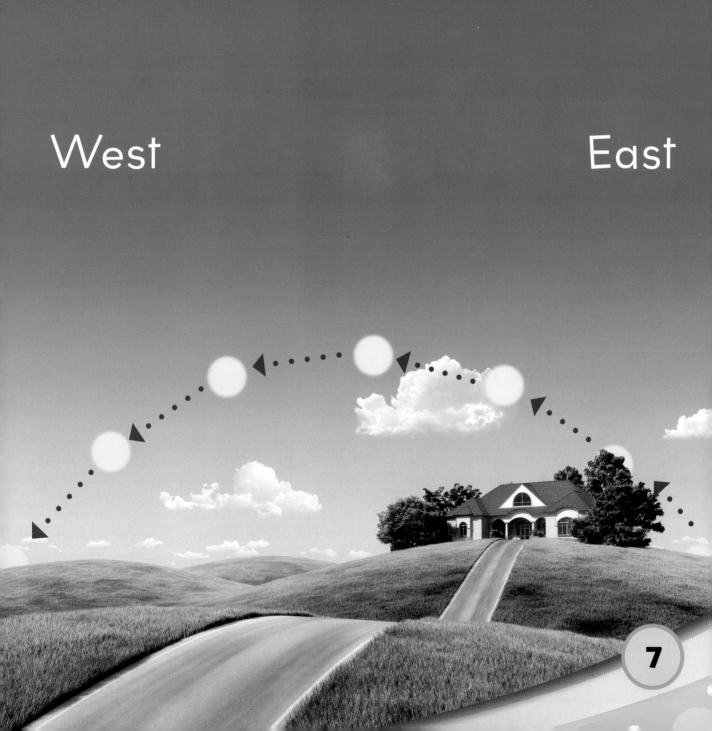

West

East

7

In the morning the Sun rises and day begins.

In the evening the Sun sets and night begins.

Night is here. The **Moon** rises.

Some nights we see a half Moon.

Some nights we see a **slice** of the Moon.

Sometimes we even see the Moon during the day!

Which do you like best?
Day or night?

SHOW what you know

1. Where does the Sun rise? In the East or West?

2. How does the Moon look different each night?

3. What are some things we see in the sky?

Picture Glossary

day (DAY):
This is the time when the sky is light, between sunrise and sunset.

Moon (MOON):
The natural satellite that moves around the Earth once each month.

night (NITE):
This is the time when the sky appears dark. It is the time between sunset and sunrise.

planet (PLAN-it):
A planet is one of the nine large bodies circling the Sun.

slice (SLISE):
A small piece cut from something larger. Sometimes the Moon appears to be just a slice.

Sun (SUHN):
The star that Earth and other planets in our solar system revolve around.

Index

Websites

www.nasa.gov/audience/forkids/kidsclub/flash/index.
html
www.kids.nineplanets.org/intro.htm
www.lpi.usra.edu/education/skytellers/day_night.
shtml

About the Author

Conrad J. Storad is the award-winning author of more than 30 books for young readers. He writes about animals, creepy crawlers, and planets. He was a magazine editor at Arizona State University for 25 years. Conrad lives in Tempe, Arizona with his wife Laurie and their miniature wiener dog, Sophia.